Wetlands

by Shirley W. Gray

Content Adviser: Terrence E. Young Jr., M.Ed., M.L.S.,
Jefferson Parish (La.) Public Schools

Reading Adviser: Dr. Linda D. Labbo,
Department of Reading Education, College of Education,
The University of Georgia

COMPASS POINT BOOKS

Minneapolis, Minnesota

Compass Point Books
3722 West 50th Street, #115
Minneapolis, MN 55410

Visit Compass Point Books on the Internet at *www.compasspointbooks.com* or e-mail your request
to *custserv@compasspointbooks.com*

Photographs ©: Stan Osolinski/FPG International, cover; Mary Clay/Colephoto, 4; Photri-Microstock, 5; Ryan C.
Taylor/Tom Stack and Associates, 6; Robert McCaw, 7; Visuals Unlimited/ H.A. Miller, 8; Index Stock Imagery, 9; Gary
Milburn/Tom Stack and Associates, 10; Root Resources/Kohout Productions, 11; Visuals Unlimited/Carol and Don Spencer,
12; Visuals Unlimited/ Wally Eberhart, 13; Robert McCaw, 14; Ryan C. Taylor/Tom Stack and Associates, 15; International
Stock/Mary McCulley, 16; Visuals Unlimited/Kirtley-Perkins, 17; David Young/Tom Stack and Associates, 18; Root
Resources/John Kohout, 19; Root Resources/Mary A. Root, 20; Robert McCaw, 21, 22, 23, 24, 25; Unicorn Stock
Photos/Bernard Hehl, 26; Brian Parker/Tom Stack and Associates, 27; Joe McDonald/Tom Stack and Associates, 28, 30;
Robert McCaw, 31; Index Stock Imagery, 32; Robert McCaw, 33; Visuals Unlimited/William J. Weber, 34; Visuals
Unlimited/John D. Cunningham, 35; Mark Stack/Tom Stack and Associates, 36; Root Resources/Jim Nachel, 37; John
Flower/Colephoto, 38; David and Tess Young/Tom Stack and Associates, 39; Photri-Microstock/Jeff Greenberg, 40; North
Wind Picture Archives, 41; Root Resources/Pat Wadecki, 42; Keith J. Whittington/Colephoto, 43.

Editors: E. Russell Primm and Emily J. Dolbear
Photo Researcher: Svetlana Zhurkina
Photo Selector: Dawn Friedman
Design: Bradfordesign, Inc.

Library of Congress Cataloging-in-Publication Data
Gray, Shirley W.
    Wetlands / by Shirley W. Gray.
       p. cm. — (First reports)
    Includes bibliographical references and index.
    Summary: Examines swamps, marshes, and other kinds of wetlands, plants and animals that
live there, and threats to the biome.
    ISBN 0-7565-0025-7 (hardcover : lib. bdg.)
    1. Wetland ecology—Juvenile literature. 2. Wetlands—Juvenile literature. [1. Wetland ecology.
2. Ecology. 3. Wetlands.] I. Title. II. Series.
    QH541.5.M3 G73 2000
    577.68—dc21   00-008536

Table of Contents

What Is a Wetland?

A **wetland** is any area of land that is underwater for at least part of the year. Water is always at or near the surface of the ground in a wetland.

▲ *A kind of wetland called a marsh, in Bear Lake National Wildlife Refuge, Idaho*

▲ *A large wetland in Northern Territory, Australia*

Some wetlands are huge, but others are only about the size of a room in your house. Wetlands are often found near lakes, ponds, rivers, and the ocean.

▲ *A saltwater marsh in Assateague Island National Seashore, Maryland*

The water in a wetland may also come from rain or melting snow. The water in some wetlands comes from deep under the ground.

▲ *A yellow-headed blackbird perches on a cattail in a freshwater marsh.*

A Look at Bogs

Have you ever heard someone talk about a **bog** or a **swamp** or a **marsh**? Bogs, swamps, and marshes are all wetlands.

Bogs are common in regions with cool climates. Large bogs are found in Canada as well as in northern

▲ A peat bog

▲ *Harvesting cranberries in a Massachusetts bog*

parts of the United States and northern Europe. Bogs are not usually found near rivers, lakes, or the ocean, though. The water in a bog comes from rain or melted snow.

The **soil** in a bog is damp and lacks the food that a living thing needs to grow. Most plants cannot grow under these conditions, but peat moss can. It is the most common plant in a bog.

▲ *This bog in Indonesia was created to grow rice.*

In most parts of the world, plants **decay**, or break down, when they die. As time passes, they become part of the soil. But when peat moss and other bog plants die, they do not decay. Instead they build up and form huge piles on top of the bog. These piles of dead plants are called **peat**. Sometimes the peat is so thick that the roots of bog plants cannot reach the soil.

In some parts of northern Europe, people dig up the peat in bogs. Then they dry it out and burn it to heat their homes. Sometimes when people dig into bogs, they find signs of ancient times. Objects do not decay in bogs, so it is possible to find things that are thousands of years old. In bogs in northern

Europe, scientists have found ancient clothing, tools, food—and even human bod-ies.

A few of the plants we eat grow well in bogs. Farmers often

▲ *Tamarack Bog in northern Wisconsin*

build bogs in order to grow cranberries and wild rice. The roots of these plants absorb food from water rather than from soil.

Marshes and Swamps

▲ *Reeds growing in a Florida marsh*

The soil in a marsh is covered with water almost all the time. The soil is so wet that trees cannot grow in a marsh. Marshes form along the shores of many lakes and rivers.

Reeds, bulrushes, and cattails usually grow in and around these freshwater marshes. Water lilies and duckweed sometimes grow on top of the water. Near the ocean, some saltwater

▲ *Rushes*

▲ *Red maple trees growing in a Canadian swamp*

marshes form. Many kinds of grasses grow in saltwater marshes that form near the ocean.

Only some parts of a swamp are underwater all
year long. In the parts that are not always covered
with water, the soil is dry enough for trees, bushes,
and vines to grow. Maple trees and oak trees can
grow on land that is not always flooded. Cypress trees

▲ *Cypress trees in the swamps of Louisiana*

and tupelo trees grow in swamps in the southern United States.

Some swamps are deep enough for flat-bottom boats. These boats are powered by pushing a long pole against the ground. Airboats can skim the surface of swamps, traveling at fast speeds.

▲ *An airboat*

Why Are Wetlands Important?

▲ *Man-made canals in the coastal wetlands of Louisiana*

During heavy rains, a wetland absorbs water like a sponge. When the rain ends, the water slowly drains out of the wetland. This keeps nearby areas from flooding. During ocean storms, saltwater wetlands absorb huge waves and prevent nearby roads and buildings from being damaged.

▲ *An aerial view of a salt marsh on Florida's west coast*

When water flows through a wetland, plants and **bacteria** remove dangerous chemicals from the water. Wetland soil often removes tiny pieces of broken-up rock from the water. The water that leaves a wetland is much cleaner than the water that flowed in.

Many animals live in or near a wetland. Many birds and mammals depend on wetlands for food. Frogs and salamanders lay their eggs in wetlands. And thousands of insects spend their whole life in a wetland. Scientists have found more than forty different kinds of mosquitoes in the wetlands of southern Florida.

▲ A mosquito feeding

Wetland Birds

▲ *A little blue heron hunting crawfish*

Birds that live in marshes and swamps have special features that help them live in these watery places. Egrets, flamingos, and herons have long slender legs so they can wade in swamps. They use their beaks like spears to catch frogs, fish, and snakes.

▲ *A great egret*

Many kinds of ducks and geese live in wetlands too. Canada geese live in the wetlands of Canada and the northern United States in the summer. In

▲ A Canada goose and her young nest on a beaver house.

autumn, they migrate to southern wetlands. You may have seen them flying in a V-formation and heard them honking loudly.

Amphibians and Reptiles

▲ *A green frog, a wetland amphibian*

Wetlands are important to frogs, salamanders, turtles, alligators, and snakes. Frogs and toads are **amphibians**. Amphibians hatch from eggs laid in the water or on wet ground. Young amphibians look like fat little fish. They have no legs and a long tail. They breathe

▲ *A spring peeper*

through gills. After a few weeks, they grow legs and begin to breathe through lungs. Soon they will spend the rest of their lives on land.

Peepers are small frogs that live in wooded swamps. You have probably heard them calling for mates in the spring. These light-brown frogs use the sticky pads on their toes to cling to bushes and trees.

Many salamanders spend most of their adult lives in forests hidden beneath logs, rocks, and leaves. They eat insects, snails, and worms. Most salamanders have brightly colored skin. Their coloring warns enemies to stay away.

Turtles, snakes, and alligators are **reptiles**. They lay their eggs on land, but often depend on wetlands for

▲ *Midland painted turtles are reptiles that live in wetlands.*

▲ An American alligator

food. The painted turtle is found in many wetlands. On warm, sunny mornings, it sits on rocks and logs.

Alligators live in swamps and marshes in warm parts of the world. They have long, dark, flat bodies and giant mouths with rows of long, sharp teeth. They eat fish, turtles, crayfish, crabs, and anything else they can catch.

▲ *An alligator almost hidden by duckweed*

▲ *A cottonmouth snake in a Florida swamp*

Snakes are at home in swamps and marshes too. Large black water snakes swim in the shallow water and then lie about on logs in the sun. Cottonmouths are poisonous snakes that live in swamps. They eat fish and frogs.

Wetland Mammals

▲ A mink

Many kinds of mammals live in wetlands. Raccoons, beavers, muskrats, minks, and river otters are common mammals in North American swamps and marshes.

River otters love to play. Like many other wetland creatures, otters make their home in burrows, or holes in the ground. They build slides in the muddy river-banks near their burrows so that they can escape into the water quickly if an enemy comes near. They enjoy playing on the slides, chasing one another up and down the muddy slopes.

▲ *A muskrat swimming*

▲ *A river otter*

Beavers cut down trees with their sharp front teeth. They use the fallen trees to build dams in rivers, streams, and brooks. Beavers live in a den underneath their dam and use a hidden underwater door to escape from danger.

▲ *A beaver pushing mud and twigs onto its dam*

The Florida Everglades

▲ *The Everglades*

Most of Florida was once covered by wetlands. During the 1900s, however, many people moved to Florida. They drained many of the wetlands so that they could build houses on the land. They also built dams and canals to keep their neighborhoods from flooding.

When the land was changed, less water flowed into

▲ *Trees growing on a hammock, or island of dry land, in the Everglades*

the remaining wetlands. And some of the water that did flow into the wetlands now carried dangerous chemicals from factories and homes. As a result, many kinds of wetland plants and animals died.

Today only one large wetland area exists in Florida. It is a huge marsh called the Everglades. In many parts of the Everglades, the water is covered by sawgrass. Small islands of dry land called hammocks

▲ *Grass, sawgrass, and palmetto in the Everglades*

▲ *Red mangrove trees*

are scattered throughout the Everglades. Forests of cypress, oaks, and palms grow on these hammocks. Other kinds of trees also thrive in the Everglades. Mangrove trees and pine trees grow in parts of the wetland.

Today, people understand the importance of protecting wetlands. They have built canals and dams that let water flow naturally through the Everglades. Scientists are trying to raise many wetland animals in zoos and then return them to the Everglades. Thanks to these efforts, the Everglades is making a comeback.

▲ *A Florida panther in its native swamp*

▲ Tamiami Canal, an irrigation control canal in the Everglade

▲ *Tamiami Canal, an irrigation control canal in the Everglade*

Part of the Everglades has been made into a national park. People can visit Everglades National Park, but no one can build on the land or hunt the animals there.

The Future of Wetlands

▲ *The entire city of Boston, shown here in the 1630s, is built on land that was once coastal wetlands.*

The Florida Everglades is not the only wetland area that has been damaged by humans. During the 1700s and 1800s, settlers in the American West drained more than half of the wetlands in the United States.

▲ *The nutrea is a South American rodent that destroys swamps by eating water plants, roots and all.*

Today people know that we need wetlands. They give us safe drinking water and prevent flooding. They also provide a home for many endangered plants and animals. Some scientists believe that wetlands may help keep the temperature on Earth steady. The United States has passed laws to protect wetlands. People in other countries are also trying to save these important areas.

In the future, some wetlands will be destroyed as cities and towns grow. When this happens, the builders will have to pay for new wetlands to be created in another place. That way, wetlands can still do their job and the creatures of the wetlands will still have a place to live.

▲ A freshwater coastal marsh in Florida

Glossary

amphibians—animals that live part of their life in water and part on land

bacteria—tiny living things so small that can only be seen with a microscope

bog—a wetland in a cool place

decay—to break down and become part of the soil

marsh—a wetland that is covered with water for most of the year and has no trees

peat—a pile of dead plant material that builds up on top of a bog

reptiles—horny-scaled animals unable to produce their own body heat

soil—a mixture of broken-up rocks and bits of decaying plants and animals

swamp—a wetland that dries up for part of the year and has trees

wetland—an area of land that is underwater for at least part of the year

Did You Know?

- About 80 percent of all birds live in wetlands for at least part of the year.

- Wetland plants have very shallow roots and hollow stems.

- Florida, Wisconsin, and Maine have the most wetlands in the United States.

- Red maples are the most common trees in wetlands.

At a Glance

Location: All over the world

Amount of rain or snow each year: Varies

Description: Low, flat land covered with water for at least part of the year

Common animals: Muskrats, beavers, deer, rabbits

Common plants: Mosses, cattails, horsetails, bulrushes, trees, shrubs

Want to Know More?

At the Library

Cone, Molly. *Squishy, Misty, Damp and Muddy: The In-Between World of Wetlands.* San Francisco: Sierra Club Books for Children, 1996.

Dunphy, Madeleine. *Here Is the Wetland.* New York: Hyperion Books for Children, 1996.

Luenn, Nancy. *Squish!: A Wetland Walk.* New York: Atheneum, 1994.

McLeish, Ewan. *Wetlands.* New York: Thomson Learning, 1996.

On the Web

The Evergreen Project: Wetlands
http://mbgnet.mobot.org/fresh/wetlands/index.htm
For information about what wetlands are and why they are important

Office of Wetlands, Oceans, and Watersheds
http://www.epa.gov/OWOW/index.html
For information from the Environmental Protection Agency about bodies of water, pollution, and clean water

Through the Mail

Soil and Water Conservation Society
7515 NE Ankeny Road
Ankeny, IA 50021
For more information about soil and water management and the environment

On the Road

Everglades National Park
40001 State Road 9336
Homestead, FL 33034-6733
305/242-7700
To visit one of the largest and most interesting wetlands in the world

Index

About the Author

Shirley W. Gray received her bachelor's degree in education from the University of Mississippi and her master's degree in technical writing from the University of Arkansas. She teaches writing and works as a science writer and editor. Shirley W. Gray lives with her husband and two sons in Little Rock, Arkansas.